NO, Calvin!

By Shondra M. Quarles

Illustrated by Hatice Bayramogul

Dedication

This book is dedicated to educators who were faced with the challenge of teaching scholars on campus during the unprecedented COVID-19 pandemic of 2020.

Calvin's teacher always said...

TEMPERATURE
CHECK

“No, Calvin!”

"NOooo,
Calvin!"

ACHOO!!

"Calvin, NO!"

"CALVIN!"

“NOoooooo!”

"Ewwww,
NO!"

“No! No! No!”

HAND
SANITIZER

"No, Calvin!"

"YES, Calvin.
I love you,
too!"

EYE
TEACHING

The End

Books by Shondra M. Quarles

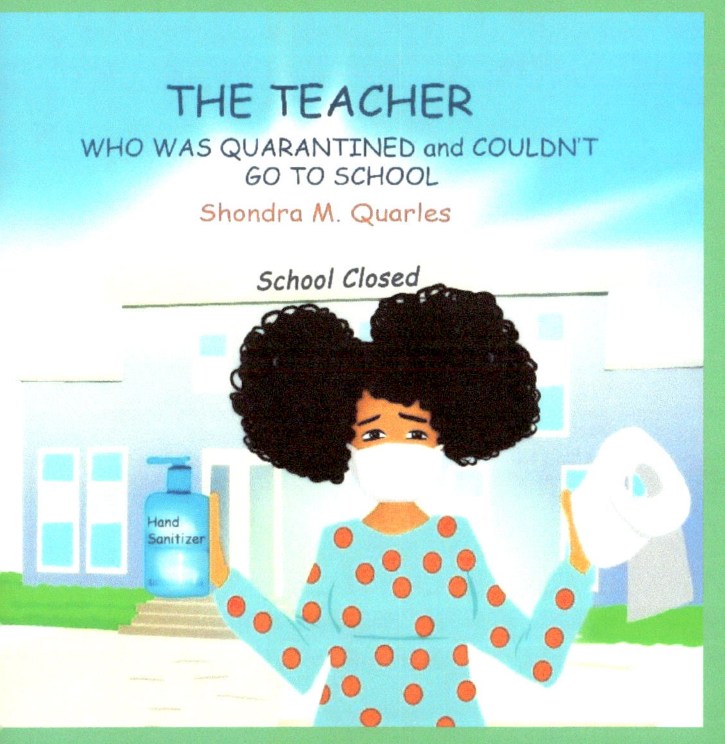

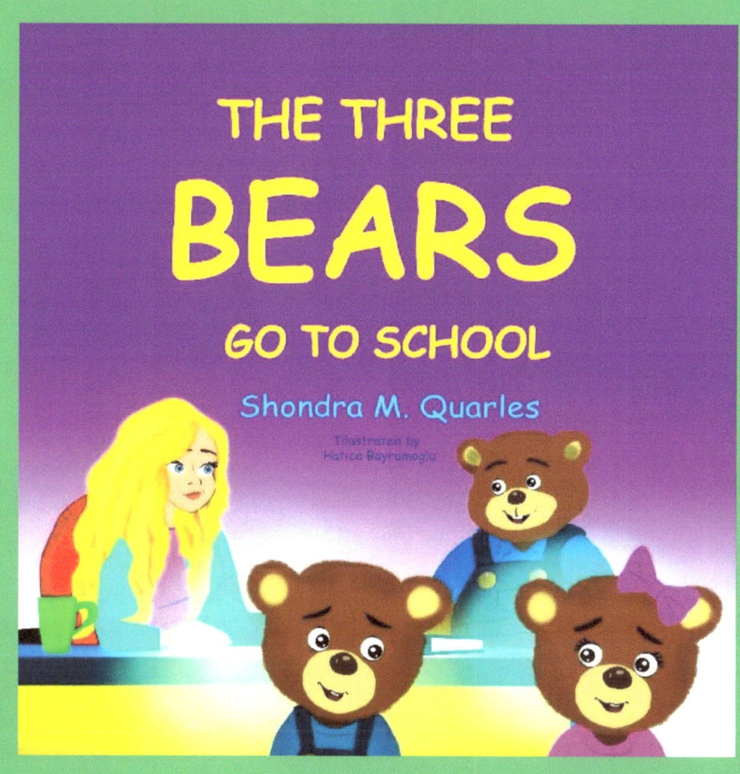

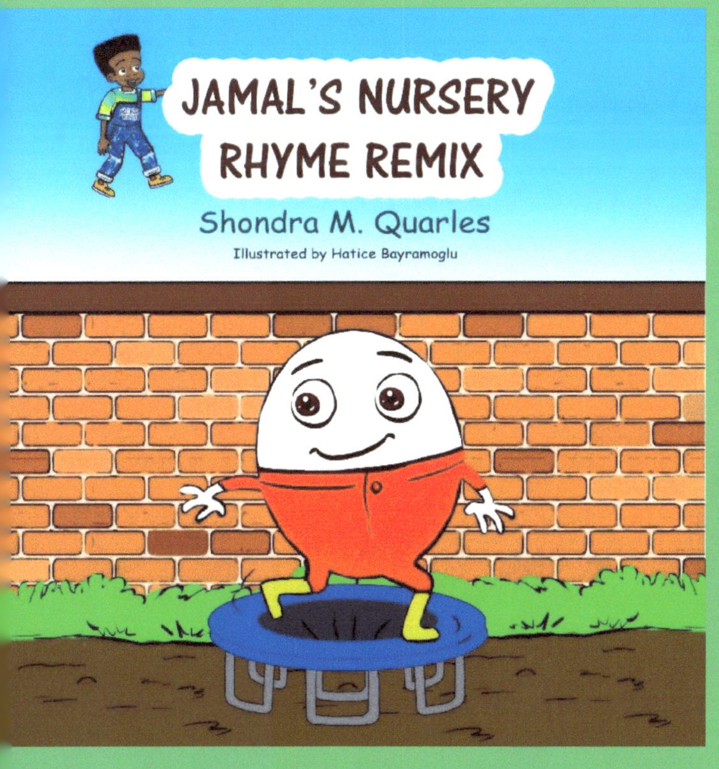

Shondra M. Quarles is an early childhood educator and children's book author who resides in Dallas. In 2014, Ms. Quarles' students inspired her to write and self-publish her first e-book titled *Kindergartner Wisdom: The Best Advice I Ever Got Came from Kindergartners*. Shondra later went on to publish her first paperback book titled *The Teacher Who Didn't Want to go to School, in 2016*. This book earned her a prestigious award from the National Celebrity Educators for authoring a book about teachers. *The Teacher Who Didn't Want to go to School* was also a children's book finalist for the 2017 and 2018 Indie Author Legacy Awards.

In 2017, Shondra co-authored a book about diversity titled *Trees*.

In 2018, she published *Black Lives Matter: A Picture Book for Kids* and *My Black is Beautiful*. Both books were written to promote self-love.

Shondra went on to be a featured author at the 2018 NAACP Convention, and her books were featured at the 2018 Essence Music Festival.

Curly Hair, Don't Care, was written in 2019 to encourage children to be proud of their natural hair. Other 2019 publications include *Young King* and *Fati's Garden*. *Young King* is a book of affirmations for young boys, and *Fati's Garden* follows a young girl who discovers the power of planting seeds.

Shondra's most recent publications are *The Three Bears go to School* and *The Teacher Who Was Quarantined and Couldn't go to School*. You can follow her writing journey on all social media platforms @eyeheartteaching.

www.ingramcontent.com/pod-product-compliance
Lightning Source LLC
Chambersburg PA
CBHW042128110726
48006CB00003B/807